A LESSON
BEFORE DYING

Ernest J. Gaines

EDITORIAL DIRECTOR Justin Kestler
EXECUTIVE EDITOR Ben Florman
DIRECTOR OF TECHNOLOGY Tammy Hepps

SERIES EDITORS Boomie Aglietti, John Crowther, Justin Kestler
MANAGING EDITOR Vince Janoski

WRITER Julio Machado
EDITORS Jesse Hawkes, Emma Chastain

This edition published by Spark Publishing

Spark Publishing
A Division of SparkNotes LLC
120 Fifth Avenue, 8th Floor
New York, NY 10011

Please submit all comments and questions or report errors to www.sparknotes.com/errors

Library of Congress Catalog-in-Publication Data available upon request

Printed in China

ISBN 1-58663-476-3

INTRODUCTION:
STOPPING TO BUY
SPARKNOTES ON A
SNOWY EVENING

Whose words these are you *think* you know.
Your paper's due tomorrow, though;
We're glad to see you stopping here
To get some help before you go.

Lost your course? You'll find it here.
Face tests and essays without fear.
Between the words, good grades at stake:
Get great results throughout the year.

Once school bells caused your heart to quake
As teachers circled each mistake.
Use SparkNotes and no longer weep,
Ace every single test you take.

Yes, books are lovely, dark, and deep,
But only what you grasp you keep,
With hours to go before you sleep,
With hours to go before you sleep.

CONTENTS

CONTEXT

ERNEST J. GAINES WAS BORN on a Louisiana plantation in 1933 in the midst of the Great Depression. He began working the fields when he was nine, digging potatoes for fifty cents a day. He spent most of his childhood with his aunt, Augusteen Jefferson, a determined woman who had no legs but who managed to take care of her family. Gaines considered her the most courageous person he ever knew. At age fifteen, Gaines moved to Vallejo, California, where he joined his parents, who had moved there during World War II. In Vallejo, Gaines discovered the public library. Since he could not find many books written about African-Americans, he decided to write his own. A few years later, he enrolled at San Francisco State University and took writing courses at Stanford University.

In 1964 Gaines published his first novel, *Catherine Carmier*. He published the novel *Of Love and Dust* three years later, followed by a short story collection entitled *Bloodline* (1968) and another entitled *A Long Day in November* (1971). He received little attention for these efforts, but felt happy about his progress as a writer. In 1971 Gaines completed one of his most famous novels, *The Autobiography of Miss Jane Pittman*. The novel follows the life of a fictional woman, Jane Pittman, who is born a slave and lives to see the black militancy of the 1960s. After the critical and financial success of *The Autobiography of Miss Jane Pittman*, Gaines published several more novels on the topic closest to his own heart: the black communities of Louisiana. The most successful of these was *A Lesson Before Dying*, which was nominated for the Pulitzer Prize and, in 1993, won the National Book Critics Circle Award.

Gaines's novel investigates the difficulties facing blacks in the rural South during the 1940s, but the historical context of the novel spans almost a century. Following the Civil War and Reconstruction, the Jim Crow Era commenced in the 1880s and continued through the turn of the century and up until 1964. This era contained the systematic destruction of black farmers in the South at the hands of resentful whites who sought to undermine black entitlement to property, animals, financial support, and even wages. The Jim Crow Era also brought with it severe segregation laws that affected every area of life and the development of white racist orga-

2 ❧ ERNEST J. GAINES

nizations, such as the Ku Klux Klan, which terrorized black communities.

As a result, between one and two million black farmers left the South during the first Great Migration from 1914 to 1930, in search of work in northern cities where factory owners promised, but never provided, high-wage jobs. In the 1940s, with the outbreak of World War II, a second Great Migration brought black farmers from the rural areas in the South to the urban, industrial areas—primarily in the northern and western United States—in search of higher-paying jobs in the burgeoning industrial economy. The second wave of migration from the rural countryside to the cities brought greater success, if only relatively. Between 1910 and 1970, more than six million blacks left the South.

A Lesson Before Dying highlights the tension inherent in the lives of African-Americans during the 1940s. Gaines highlights how the pull away from the South divided blacks from their heritage and their roots, stranding them in a world where, it seemed, one had to look, talk, and act white in order to succeed. At the same time, however, remaining connected with one's roots—with the rural South— meant having to live in a world fraught with Jim Crow laws and racial segregation (which remained in existence until the Civil Rights Act of 1964 and the Voting Rights Act of 1965). Racial violence and hatred pervaded all sectors of American society, but were felt most acutely in the rural South.

Plot Overview

GRANT WIGGINS HAS BEEN TEACHING on a plantation outside Bayonne, Louisiana, for several years when a slow-witted man named Jefferson is convicted of murder and sentenced to death. Jefferson claims he is innocent of the crime. He says he was on his way to a bar, but changed his mind and decided to tag along with two men who were on their way to a liquor store. Upon arriving there, the two men began arguing with the storeowner, and a shootout ensued. The storeowner and the two men died, and Jefferson remained at the scene of the crime. He was arrested and tried for murder. Jefferson's lawyer argues in court that Jefferson is nothing but a poor fool, hardly more worthwhile than a hog, and therefore incapable of plotting such a scheme. The jury quickly brings back a guilty verdict.

Upon hearing the lawyer's speech, Jefferson's godmother, Miss Emma, resolves to help Jefferson die like a man, not a hog. She asks Grant to help her, knowing that he will resist. Grant left many years prior to attend college, and he returned an educated man. He deplores the injustices done to his fellow black men, but he does not want to get involved in Jefferson's case. However, after considerable pressure from his aunt, Tante Lou, he agrees to try to help Jefferson. Grant, Miss Emma, and Grant's aunt go to visit Jefferson in his cell, and they discover that he too heard the lawyer's words and has taken them to heart. Silent and moody, Jefferson resists Grant's feeble attempts to reach him. The three visitors spend an uncomfortable hour in the cell and then leave.

During the next few visits, Jefferson continues to frustrate Grant's attempts to communicate. When Grant attempts to teach Jefferson about dignity, Jefferson insists that dignity is for "you-mans," not hogs. He eats and snuffles in imitation of a hog and tries to anger Grant with stubbornness and malice, but Grant maintains his patience. Each hour-long visit ends in failure, but Grant continues to try to reach Jefferson. On his fourth visit, Grant sparks a conversation with Jefferson about his final meal. Jefferson admits that he wants a gallon of vanilla ice cream because, although he loves ice cream, he has never had more than a thimbleful at a time. This admission begins to break down the barrier between the two men. Grant borrows money from some townspeople and buys Jefferson a small radio. On his next visit, he brings Jefferson a notebook and asks him to write down whatever thoughts come to his mind. Jefferson promises to do so, and by Grant's next visit, Jefferson has filled most of a page with thoughts concerning the difference between hogs and men.

Grant's relationships with his girlfriend Vivian and with Reverend Ambrose begin to intensify. Despite her love for Grant, Vivian dislikes his tendency to think only of himself, showing little regard for her needs. Grant uses Vivian to escape the troubles of his life, and he continually suggests that they run away from their hometown and their past in the South. The Reverend Ambrose, himself unable to reach Jefferson, urges Grant to put aside his atheistic beliefs and help save not just Jefferson's character, but his soul. The Reverend declares that Grant must learn to tell lies for the good of others.

Grant focuses his energy on Jefferson and tries to explain the importance of Jefferson's death. Jefferson asks Grant if he believes in heaven and Grant replies that he does not, although he qualifies this remark by saying that his atheism does not make him a good man. In fact, Grant says, Jefferson will save even Grant's atheistic soul if he carries the cross for the sinners on earth. Grant explains that the black community in the quarter has spent centuries enslaved to white men, and that when Jefferson's attorney called him a hog, he attacked the will and intelligence of the entire black society. In consequence, Jefferson now has the opportunity to stand up for his community. He has become a symbol to his people, and the manner in which he faces his death will bear on their self-confidence and potential.

Over the next few weeks, Jefferson continues to write in his journal. In March, the governor of Louisiana sets the execution date for two weeks after Easter. As news of Jefferson's impending death spreads through the town, more and more people begin to visit him. Young children and old men, strangers and friends, all come to Jefferson's cell to speak to him. The onslaught of attention makes Jefferson begin to understand the enormity of the task that Grant has given him. He realizes that he has become much more than an ordinary man and that his death will represent much more than an ordinary death. Elated by Jefferson's progress, Grant nevertheless dreads the execution day, when that progress will be tested.

Grant cannot bring himself to attend the execution, for he has grown very close to Jefferson. At the time the execution is scheduled to take place, he orders his students to kneel by their desks in honor of Jefferson. He steps outside the classroom, distressed and bewil-

dered. He knows he should have attended the execution. A few minutes later, a deputy comes down from the courthouse and informs
Grant that the execution is over. He assures Grant that Jefferson was
the bravest man in the room that morning. Grant looks out over the
town, numb and heavyhearted, and discovers that he is crying.

CHARACTER LIST

Grant Wiggins The protagonist and narrator of the novel, an elementary school teacher in his mid-twenties. Grant is intelligent and willful, but also somewhat hypocritical and depressed. A life spent in a segregated, racist community has made him bitter. He has no faith in himself, his society, or his church. He does not believe anything will ever change and thinks escape is the only option. He fears committing himself to a fight he cannot win. This defeatist attitude makes him shun responsibility, and he resents Tante Lou and Miss Emma for forcing him to help Jefferson. Over the course of the novel, however, he learns to accept responsibility for his own life, for his relations with other people, and for his role as an educator and agent of change in his needy community.

Jefferson A sincere, sensitive, young black man of below-average intelligence. When his lawyer calls him a "hog," Jefferson takes the insult to heart and begins to consider himself powerless in the white-dominated society. He becomes sullen and withdrawn, accepting a living death and therefore becoming a dark symbol of his oppressed people. Grant attempts to heal Jefferson's pain. He believes that Jefferson can stop symbolizing the troubles of the black community and start symbolizing positive change.

Tante Lou Grant's aunt, and a deeply religious woman. Tante Lou resents Grant's cynical atheism, perhaps because she feels it reflects badly on the way she raised him. Tante Lou took in Grant when his parents moved away and became a mother figure to him. Although she lives a troubled life under a harsh, racist system, she finds freedom for her soul in the church, her family, her dignity, and her pride.

Miss Emma Jefferson's godmother. Miss Emma possesses great faith in God. After hearing Jefferson's lawyer call Jefferson a hog, she becomes obsessed with ensuring that Jefferson dies "like a man." Miss Emma expresses her emotions freely and demonstrates her strength and resolve during Jefferson's trial and incarceration.

Reverend Ambrose The fiery, self-righteous leader of the black quarter's religious community, and Grant's primary foil in the novel. Reverend Ambrose believes that true faith in God shields the believer against oppression. Ambrose believes that Grant is foolish for forsaking his religion and that Grant will have a sinful influence on Jefferson. Jefferson connects only with Grant, and the Reverend cannot convince Grant to attempt to save Jefferson's soul. In his conversations with Grant, the Reverend reveals his belief that lying is a necessary component of survival, especially for Southern blacks struggling to live.

Vivian Grant's beautiful, loving, and intelligent girlfriend. Vivian is a schoolteacher at the black Catholic school in Bayonne. She is married and has two children, but is in the process of divorcing her husband. She wants to hide her relationship with Grant for fear her husband will use it to justify taking the children away from her. She distrusts Grant because, in his self-centered way, he pressures her to forsake her community.

Matthew Antoine Grant's primary school teacher and predecessor as the quarter's schoolteacher. Antoine dies before the events in the novel begin, but his influence on Grant is felt throughout the novel. His defeated, resentful cynicism contributed to Grant's bitterness.

Sheriff Guidry An authoritarian man who runs the prison in Bayonne. Guidry resents anyone who trespasses on his domain, especially blacks like Grant and Miss Emma. He provides blacks with a modicum of freedom and opportunity while maintaining an overarching, white authoritarian superstructure.

Paul The sheriff's deputy at the Bayonne jail, he is the only white in the novel who truly sympathizes with the black struggle in the South.

Henri Pichot A stubborn white man with a sense of duty, he owns the plantation where Grant spent his childhood. Pichot is not a bad man, but he enjoys his position of power in the quarter. He cherishes the status quo because it allows him to feel superior to people. Like many of his white peers, he causes harm simply by his unwillingness to change.

Mr. Joseph Morgan The white superintendent of schools. Like Pichot, Dr. Joseph knowingly maintains the status quo: black oppression under a fundamentally racist system. A hypocrite, Mr. Joseph presents a façade of benevolence, but he actually believes that although black children should receive a small amount of religious and patriotic education, they should primarily work the fields as farm hands.

CHARACTER LIST

ANALYSIS OF MAJOR CHARACTERS

GRANT WIGGINS

The protagonist of the novel, Grant is the son of cane-cutters who labored on a Louisiana plantation. He grows up working in a menial job, but makes his escape and goes to college. He returns to his hometown a secular, educated man, distanced from his downtrodden black community. College has given him a more sophisticated perspective and an educated way of thinking and speaking. Yet despite the changes in Grant, white people still consider him inferior. Their shoddy treatment outrages Grant, but he says nothing and does nothing. He feels rage at the whites for treating him badly and rage at himself for taking the treatment lying down. This rage, bottled up in Grant, turns to bitterness, cynicism, and self-absorption. He feels he cannot help his community, and in order to stop this failure from paining him, he removes himself from the people he loves, looking on them with contempt and deciding that, since they are beyond hope, he cannot be blamed for failing to help them.

Grant's perspective changes over the course of the novel as a result of his visits to Jefferson and his interactions with Vivian, his aunt Tante Lou, and Reverend Ambrose. He learns to love something other than himself and to strive for change without retreating into his shell of cynicism. Still, Gaines does not suggest that because Grant's attitude improves, he will be able to effect great change; he does not even suggest that Grant's attitude improves entirely. Jefferson dies nobly, but he still dies, murdered by his racist oppressors. Grant ends the novel encouraged by the changes he has seen, but depressed at the barbarity of his society. He is still afraid, he is still withdrawn from some people, and he is still sarcastic and angry. Grant's character development suggests that although great personal and societal improvement is possible, no quick fix will help a racist community, and for that reason Grant is justified in his despair.

JEFFERSON

The novel centers around Jefferson's unjust conviction and his friends' attempts to help him die with human dignity. A relatively simple man, Jefferson has spent his entire life on the plantation, working for poor wages. He has always worked without protest, believing that his place in the world is a lowly one. When Jefferson's lawyer defends Jefferson by likening him to a mindless hog, Jefferson becomes terrified and infuriated, obsessed by the possibility that he really is no better than a hog. He rages in his cell, mimicking a hog's behavior and jeering at his friends and family, or refusing to speak to them.

When Grant visits Jefferson for the first time, Jefferson is so withdrawn and sullen that Grant thinks it will be impossible to help him. Jefferson does change with Grant's help, however. He begins to believe in his own worth, and he realizes his life and manner of dying might have symbolic importance for his community. Gaines casts Jefferson as a Christ figure, a man to whom people look for their own salvation. Jefferson becomes brave and thoughtful, and his journal reveals the truth that even the most woefully uneducated man can possess depths of intelligence and lyricism.

SHERIFF SAM GUIDRY

Guidry is both an archetypal white authoritarian and a decent man. Guidry voices the ignorance, hypocrisy, inertia, and racism of the people in power in the South of the 1940s. As town sheriff, Guidry has plenty of power to wield. He resents any trespasses on his sphere of influence, and he wants to maintain the status quo in his courthouse and in his society. He believes that Jefferson should be left to die in happy, animalistic ignorance. Still, as soon as Jefferson and Grant begin to transcend the roles that Guidry and other powerful whites assign for them—as soon as they cease playing the humble schoolteacher and the angry, stupid criminal—Guidry seems to sense the fragility of his position. His worldview depends upon blacks conforming to these stereotypes; when they refuse to conform, Guidry becomes unsure of his footing. Although Guidry does not repent and change, he does show signs of increasing sensitivity. His harsh exterior begins to crack and reveal a kindly, anxious streak. By the end of the novel, he treats Jefferson with something approaching respect.

TANTE LOU

Tante Lou is slightly subdued and seldom reveals her thoughts to Grant. Even by the end of the novel, we do not truly understand her. Her occasional remarks reveal her to be a spiritual woman, motivated by a powerful faith in God and in his good works. Because of her faith, Tante Lou has the hope and resilience Grant lacks, and she disapproves of Grant's cynical brand of atheism. She exudes a sense of dignity despite her position in society; she and Miss Emma dress respectably and insist upon being chauffeured in the backseat to the Pichots. Tante Lou refuses to accept the idea that she must despair just because blacks in the South remain on the bottom rung of the economic ladder. Tante Lou is a positive force in Grant's life and in the community. In some ways, she is responsible for Grant's evolution. She demands that he behave with compassion and bravery, nagging him to help Jefferson and insisting that he speak with the Pichots in order to gain visitation rights at the prison.

THEMES, MOTIFS & SYMBOLS

THEMES

Themes are the fundamental and often universal ideas explored in a literary work.

RECOGNIZING INJUSTICE AND FACING RESPONSIBILITY

Grant often criticizes his society. He bitterly resents the racism of whites, and he cannot stand to think of Jefferson's unjust conviction and imprisonment. For most of the novel, however, he does nothing to better his lot. He sarcastically claims that he teaches children to be strong men and women despite their surroundings, but he is a difficult, angry schoolmaster. Grant longs to run away and escape the society he feels will never change. Like Professor Antoine, he believes no one can change society without being destroyed in the process.

Jefferson's trial reinforces Grant's pessimistic attitude. Grant sees the wickedness of a system designed to uphold the superiority of one race over another. He sees a man struck down to the level of a hog by a few words from an attorney. He sees a judge blind to justice and a jury deaf to truth. These injustices are particularly infuriating because no one stands up to defy them. The entire town accepts Jefferson's conviction with a solemn silence. Even Grant stays silent, resisting his aunt and Miss Emma, who implore him to teach Jefferson how to regain his humanity.

During the course of the novel, however, Grant comes to realize that cynicism like his is akin to lying down and dying, and that even small victories can accumulate and produce change. Rather than looking at Jefferson as a hopeless stranger, or ridiculing him as someone who tries to make Grant feel guilty, Grant accepts Jefferson's plight as his own and begins to fight for Jefferson's salvation. He accepts his duty to the society he inhabits, thereby taking the first step toward improving that society.

REDEMPTION IN DEATH

With its consistent references to Jesus Christ and his crucifixion, this novel insists that a man's death can be a meaningful event that bolsters a community. Jefferson has led a quiet life, working as a common laborer for years and never speaking a word out of turn. When convicted for a crime he did not commit, Jefferson is initially angry and recalcitrant, acting like the animal the whites think him. Eventually, however, his death sentence liberates him, and he finds spiritual rejuvenation.

By the end of the novel, Jefferson understands that by dying like a man, he will defy the society that wrongfully accused him and convicted him not just of murder, but of being black-skinned. He knows that by refusing to bow down in his final moments, he will make his community proud. For these reasons, he walks to his execution calmly, and onlookers say he is the strongest man in the room.

THE INESCAPABLE PAST

Both Grant and Vivian are haunted by their pasts. White people treated Grant as their inferior as he was growing up. Grant deliberately severs himself from his past because thinking of it discomfits him. Vivian, however, recognizes the sway her past has over her, and she deals with it. She cannot completely embrace her relationship with Grant, in part because her husband still threatens to take her children away from her. She also realizes that their history in Bayonne means that she and Grant cannot run away from their town. Unlike Grant, she recognizes that the problems of the past will not disappear by changing geographic location. Moreover, she recognizes that Grant's wish to ignore his past is symptomatic of his inability to love his community, or to love her for that matter. Gaines suggests that only confronting racism will change it.

CONSTRUCTIVE LYING

Reverend Ambrose delivers a rousing speech to Grant asserting that black people must lie and cheat in order to survive in the racist South. They must tell themselves that heaven exists, that they are not in pain, that God is good. The reverend suggests that Grant should cease judging people for lying. After all, Grant went to college on the strength of his aunt's lies. She deceived him and herself, saying she was fine when actually she was working her fingers to the bone. Gaines suggests that racism forces men and women to compromise their ideals simply to stay alive. He suggests that if black people are not to lie down and give up in the face of an unethical system, they must sustain their sense of hope although it may require them to lie to themselves.

MOTIFS

Motifs are recurring structures, contrasts, or literary devices that can help to develop and inform the text's major themes.

SMALL DISPLAYS OF POWER

Gaines shows how racism pervades every nook and cranny of society, grinding down black people in everyday interactions. Black people are made to feel their inferiority when they are made to wait at a white person's leisure, forced to enter through the back door of a white person's house, or treated shabbily by a white salesperson. When Grant must enter Pichot's house through the back door, it is a symbolic reminder of the days of slavery, when slaves could never approach the front door. When angry, the black Reverend Ambrose wields his power over Grant by calling him "boy," using one of the pejorative terms usually employed by racist whites when referring to grown black men. Gaines suggests that such small moments of subjugation are impossible to shake off because of their cumulative oppressive effect.

CHRISTIAN IMAGERY

Jefferson becomes a Christ figure as the novel progresses. Unjustly tried and convicted, the simple-minded Jefferson dies a martyr. The mayor attempts to dispel some of the associations of Jefferson with Christ by setting the execution date for two weeks after Easter, but his awareness of the imagery simply reinforces its power. In trying to move Jefferson to die with dignity, the cynical Grant begins to think of him as a Christ figure—repenting in front of Jefferson and saying that he feels lost—but should Jefferson show him the way, he will find salvation, if not as a Christian then as a caring and active member of the community. Grant tells Vivian that only Jefferson can break the cycle of failed black men; at the end of the novel, Grant begs Jefferson's forgiveness as if speaking to a savior.

SYMBOLS

*Symbols are objects, characters, figures, or colors used to
represent abstract ideas or concepts.*

THE NOTEBOOK

The notebook represents Jefferson's reconnection with his humanity, a reconciliation facilitated by Grant. By writing down his
thoughts, Jefferson reflects upon his position in an unjust world and
begins to think seriously about his life. The notebook also symbolizes the reciprocal friendship between Grant and Jefferson. Grant
gives Jefferson the notebook, symbolizing his desire to teach Jefferson and help Jefferson teach himself. Jefferson writes in the notebook as if writing a letter to Grant, which suggests that Jefferson
looks to Grant for guidance even when alone in his cell. Finally, the
notebook symbolizes hope for future collaboration not just between
blacks, but between blacks and whites—for Paul, the white deputy,
delivers the book to Grant and asks to shake Grant's hand.

THE CHAIR

When it arrives in a large black truck, the chair in which Jefferson must
die evokes many different reactions from people in the town. The truck
drives slowly through the town, and everyone comes out to see it. Some
fear the chair. Some become nauseous looking at it or thinking about it.
Some treat it with great care and hesitate to joke about it. Others, spe-
cifically white men, joke about using it to warn black men to watch
their steps. The chair symbolizes the violence of the unjust system that
convicted Jefferson. It also represents the fear that racism instills.

THE CHURCH

The church symbolizes the hope that society will change. Miss
Emma, Tante Lou, and Reverend Ambrose believe that God helps
them—they use this belief to comfort themselves in the face of prejudice and injustice. In the reverend's eyes, when Grant uncondition-
ally rejects God and the church, he rejects the possibility that
anything can be done to improve society. Reverend Ambrose confronts Grant in Chapter 27, asking him, "You think a man can't kneel
and stand?" The reverend suggests that kneeling before God does not
humble people, it gives them dignity. When Grant recognizes that his
rejection of the church stems from his own inability to engage actively
with his community, he moves closer to a dignified existence.

FOOD AND DRINK

Characters use food to symbolize their affection for one another. Miss Emma brings food for Jefferson; when he refuses to eat it, Grant takes the refusal seriously as an expression of Jefferson's anger at his family and begs him to eat in order to show Miss Emma that he loves her. When Grant becomes angry with Tante Lou, he insults her by refusing to eat her cooking. Grant offers to bring Jefferson ice cream and asks his students to gather peanuts and pecans as a gift for Jefferson. At the pivotal moment when Jefferson starts teaching Grant, he offers Grant food as a way of showing his affection.

SYMBOLS

SUMMARY & ANALYSIS

CHAPTERS 1–2

SUMMARY: CHAPTER 1

> *What justice would there be to take this life? Justice,*
> *gentlemen? Why, I would just as soon put a hog in the*
> *electric chair as this.*   *(See* QUOTATIONS, *p. 53)*

Grant Wiggins recalls the outcome of a trial. He says that he was not there, but he knew what the verdict would be. He pictures the courtroom, the judge, and the attorneys. He pictures his aunt, Tante Lou, sitting beside the defendant's godmother, Miss Emma, both watching the proceedings with solemn rigidity. Grant can picture the back of Jefferson's close-cropped black head as he sits at the defendant's table.

Grant recalls the incidents leading up to the trial. Jefferson, Grant says, was on his way to the White Rabbit Bar and Lounge when Brother and Bear, two young black men, drove up beside him and offered him a ride. The three men drove to a store, where Brother and Bear demanded that Alcee Gropé, the store owner, give them drinks on credit. Alcee refused, and the ensuing argument led to a shootout. Alcee, Brother, and Bear all died, leaving Jefferson alone in the store. Grant says Jefferson stood at the scene of the crime, confused and frightened, and took a slug of whiskey to calm his nerves. He looked around and saw the open cash register full of money. He knew that stealing was wrong, but he also knew that he would need to run, so he took some money. He had nearly reached the door when two white men walked into the store.

Grant says the prosecution argued that Jefferson had gone to the store intending to rob and kill Alcee Gropé. The prosecution claimed that Jefferson stuffed the money into his pockets and celebrated the murder by drinking some of Alcee's liquor. Grant says that Jefferson's attorney defended Jefferson by insisting that he is a boy and a fool, and therefore incapable of planning the robbery and murder. The attorney said he would rather put a hog in the electric chair than such a mindless individual. The white jury members deliberated for just a few hours before finding Jefferson guilty of robbery and murder in the first degree. A few days later, the judge sentenced Jefferson to death by electrocution.

SUMMARY: CHAPTER 2

When Grant comes home from school on the afternoon of the trial, he finds his aunt, Tante Lou, and Jefferson's godmother, Miss Emma, sitting quietly at the table. He hurries to his room. He knows they want to talk about the trial and wishes desperately to avoid the subject. For courtesy's sake, however, he goes out to the kitchen. He tries to excuse himself quickly, but they insist on talking to him. Grief-stricken, Miss Emma thinks about how Jefferson's attorney compared Jefferson to a hog. She tells Grant that she does not want Jefferson to die a hog and that she wants Grant to accompany her to the prison and teach Jefferson to die with dignity. Grant angrily refuses, insisting he can do nothing to help Jefferson. Tante Lou tells Grant that all three of them must visit Mr. Henry Pichot because his brother-in-law, the sheriff, might admit them to see Jefferson. Grant clenches his fists in fury. He wants to scream at his aunt and tell her how much he hates the town and how helpless he feels in this oppressive environment, but he knows that she would not hear him.

ANALYSIS: CHAPTERS 1–2

The first chapter opens with the novel's fundamental concern: how can justice prevail in a society dominated by a single group of people? In Jefferson's trial, the judge is white, the lawyers are white, and every member of the jury is white. Therefore, Jefferson receives a trial not by his peers, but by his oppressors. Jefferson's attorney pleads for Jefferson's innocence by appealing to white prejudices, arguing that Jefferson is as morally blank as a hog. This trial robs Jefferson of his legal rights. Because he is black in a racist society, the law will not help Jefferson. The jurors are not even asked to consider the legality of the situation. Rather, they are asked to acquit him because he is a pathetic creature.

On one hand, Gaines condemns the society as racist. To Grant, the trial is an elaborate performance with a predetermined conclusion: Jefferson will be found guilty. Grant understands that in this society, a black man is guilty until proven innocent. Under the law, the prosecution has to prove Jefferson's guilt, but under the rules of convention in this racist society, the prosecution must only concoct a vague theory based on no evidence. Jefferson's attorney defends his client not by using the evidence, but by damning Jefferson as a hog and a fool too stupid to plan such a crime. Grant's decision to stay away from the trial begins to seem not a cynical refusal to hope for a not guilty verdict, but a sensible realization that no matter what the evidence says, Jefferson will be found guilty. On the other hand, Gaines intentionally blurs the truth in this opening chapter, questioning the truth of Grant's statements. At this point, we do not know for sure what happened during the crime. Grant details several different versions of the crime even though he witnessed neither the crime nor the trial. Gaines deliberately leaves the story murky in order to suggest the murkiness of racism in America.

The opening chapter paints Grant, the narrator, as a proud black man who suffers because he lives in a racist time and place. Gaines suggests Grant might be deceiving himself, since he distances himself from Jefferson's trial and yet claims to know exactly what happened there. Although Grant says he did not attend Jefferson's trial because he knew what the verdict would be, Gaines suggests that Grant also stayed away because he willfully imposes a distance between himself and his family and community. Grant says he could have sat with his aunt and Jefferson's godmother, but he chose to separate himself from them.

Grant explains his anger toward his aunt and Miss Emma by saying that they ask him to perform a difficult, perhaps impossible, task: Miss Emma wants him to undo the effects of eighteen years of racist oppression. The huge machinery of the oppressors has ground down Jefferson, and Miss Emma wants Grant to take on this machinery and give Jefferson defiance and strength of character. Like most of the people in the audience, Miss Emma understood the racism in the defense attorney's speech and she wants to fight it.

CHAPTERS 3–5

SUMMARY: CHAPTER 3

Tante Lou, Miss Emma, and Grant arrive at the Pichot plantation. They enter through the back door and inform the maid that they wish to see Mr. Pichot. Miss Emma was the cook here for most of her life, just like her mother and grandmother before her. Grant's aunt washed and ironed, and Grant ran errands. When he left for college, he vowed never to enter this place through the back door again. After some delay, Henry Pichot and Louis Rougon enter the kitchen. Miss Emma asks Pichot to convince his brother-in-law to allow Grant to visit the prison and educate Jefferson. Pichot hesitates, and Miss Emma reminds him of all the years she spent working for his family. Pichot asks Grant what he expects to do, and Grant responds truthfully that he does not know. Grant carefully avoids being disrespectful, making sure to lower his eyes when necessary. After some cajoling, Pichot agrees to speak to his brother-in-law.

SUMMARY: CHAPTER 4

After dropping off Miss Emma, Grant informs his aunt that he will eat in town, which insults her. He drives to Bayonne. After crossing the railroad tracks and making his way down a poorly lit road into the black section of town, Grant stops at the Rainbow Club where Thelma Claiborne, the owner's wife, prepares his dinner. At Grant's request, his lighter-skinned girlfriend Vivian arrives. She sits with Grant and they talk quietly. He offers to take her and her children far away from the town, but she considers the idea unrealistic and threatens to leave the bar if he continues to speak about it. She asks him why he has not left town for good, and he replies that he wants to be with her. She calls him a liar, because he once left the town to stay with his parents in California. When Vivian asks him why he returned, Grant avoids the question. She reminds him that they cannot be so open about their love for one another until she finalizes her divorce. While dancing, Grant tells her about Jefferson's sentence. Angry and afraid, Grant wonders if he can teach Jefferson how to die when Grant himself doesn't know how to live.

SUMMARY: CHAPTER 5

The next morning, Grant returns to the plantation school where he teaches black children through the sixth grade. His school is in a church, and his desk is a table normally devoted to the Sunday collection. Grant teaches only five and a half months out of the year, because his students work in the fields the rest of the time. In a foul mood, Grant punishes his students for the slightest offenses, though they try to avoid upsetting him. After a few hours, he steps outside and surveys the homes near his school. He knows many details about the troubled lives of their inhabitants. When he returns to his classroom, he finds a student playing with an insect. He sneaks up behind the young boy and slaps him hard across the back of the head with his ruler. Furious, Grant finds himself telling the class about the task Miss Emma has set for him. He explains how Jefferson will die and says he must make Jefferson into a man, which is exactly what he is trying to do with them. Toward the end of class, a small man enters the church and informs Grant that Mr. Henri Pichot wishes to see him.

ANALYSIS: CHAPTERS 3-5

The main conflict of *A Lesson Before Dying* lies within Grant himself. Even though Grant struggles to manage in the racist white society, his primary struggle is with his own mind. As he says to Vivian, he cannot face Jefferson because he cannot face himself and his own life. Vivian exposes Grant's conflicted nature by bringing up the fact that he left the South in the past but eventually returned. Grant feels repulsed by the environment in which he grew up, but somehow he cannot bring himself to leave. Despite his statement that Vivian's presence is the reason that he remains in Bayonne, Vivian knows that there are larger issues at play here. The novel shows that Grant's pride and self-centered qualities prevent him from truly appreciating the people with whom he lives. When he finally learns how to view his family and friends positively, he becomes able to live in the South with strength and courage.

Undoubtedly, however, Grant is not completely responsible for his inability to overcome his inner conflict. Life in the South during the time of Jim Crow segregation was harrowing for blacks and Grant's vacillation between cynical confidence and despair results from his daily struggle against the forces of racism. Here, Gaines paints Grant's visit to Henri Pichot as a humiliating experience. Grant, Tante Lou, and Miss Emma have to enter Pichot's house through the servants' entrance in the back and then must wait awkwardly until Pichot deigns to see them. They talk to Pichot as servants to master, careful to appear respectful and able to appeal only to his sense of duty and generosity for help. Moreover, as Pichot oppresses blacks by making them serve and beg, the town of Bayonne oppresses them by segregating them to the back of the town. White families own the plantations and fields, and black families work them. White men run the jails, and black men rot in them. White women bear white children, and black women care for them. Gaines shows that the blacks are not only segregated, but they receive meager resources, such as electricity. The road to the black section of town is noticeably darker than the main streets with streetlights.

The inequities of racism also divide blacks from each other. Although Grant is inextricably bound to Tante Lou and Miss Emma, he is also distanced from them. He feels pressured by Tante Lou to conform to the racist expectations of the whites. He drives the women to Pichot's, yet he cannot stand living as they do, constantly submitting to white authority. He refuses Tante Lou's food in order to show his resentment and disapproval of her behavior. Grant feels both a connection to and a detachment from his pupils. He wants them to thrive, to transcend the low-class work for which they have been slated, but he expresses frustration when they do not exhibit the concentration that will help them thrive. To the extent that he wants his students to succeed and identifies with their plight, Grant is on their side. Just as his aunt angers him, however, his students anger him. He deals with them harshly, punishing them for tiny offenses and making them afraid. Although he cares for them, he frequently seems disgusted by them and convinced that they cannot make anything of themselves.

In these chapters, we see that Grant is a man divided—from his family, from his friends, from himself—due to the deeply scarring environmental influences of racism. The conflict between Grant and his community shows that while racism attempts to lump people into categories and degrade them as indistinguishable members of a particular group, human beings differ from one another. Not all blacks experience or respond to racism in the same manner, and these differences can result in conflict and misunderstanding—misunderstanding that must be healed before the family and the community can strengthen themselves against further oppression.

CHAPTERS 6–8

SUMMARY: CHAPTER 6

> *It doesn't matter anymore. Just do the best you can. But it won't matter.* (See QUOTATIONS, *p.* 54)

A maid lets Grant into the Pichot kitchen through the back door. She informs him that Mr. Pichot's brother-in-law, sheriff Sam Guidry, will arrive soon. Grant waits in the kitchen, thinking moodily about his role in Jefferson's affairs. After half an hour, Grant hears Sam Guidry and his wife Edna arrive at the front door. After another half hour, Edna enters the kitchen. She asks him many questions, but never gives him an opportunity to answer. She drinks bourbon and she says she feels sorry about Jefferson and the murder. After another hour and fifteen minutes, Sheriff Sam Guidry, Henri Pichot, Louis Rougon, and a fat man walk into the kitchen. Guidry asks Grant how long he has been waiting, and Grant tells him flatly, "About two and a half hours." Grant realizes he should have grinned and said, "Not long," but his anger and pride prevented him from being submissive. Guidry asks what Grant wants to do with Jefferson, and Grant politely answers that he does not know. After a while, the sheriff informs him that he can see Jefferson in a few weeks, although he thinks Grant's efforts will fail and Grant should let Jefferson die a "contented hog." Moreover, the sheriff says that Grant will lose his visiting privileges if he "aggravates" Jefferson.

SUMMARY: CHAPTER 7

During the next few weeks, Grant awaits the annual visit by the superintendent of schools. He makes sure that his students appear clean and well behaved, since the superintendent could arrive at any moment. When the superintendent, Dr. Joseph Morgan, finally arrives, Grant notes Dr. Morgan's heaviness and the difficulty with which he gets out of his car. Grant escorts Dr. Morgan to his own desk and then stands with his class. Dr. Morgan calls up several of the boys and girls, choosing the most obviously self-conscious or problematic students. He checks their teeth and asks them to recite Bible verses. He is angry yet vindicated when one young boy fails to recite his lessons properly. Grant thinks of the similarity between Dr. Morgan's inspection and slave masters' inspections. Dr. Morgan lectures the class on the virtues of good nutrition, hygiene, and physical labor, but compliments Grant on his class. Grant complains to the superintendent that most of the school's shabby books are hand-me-downs from white schools. This grievance annoys the superintendent, who says that white schools struggle too. Before leaving, Dr. Morgan suggests that Grant put the children to work in the fields to earn money.

SUMMARY: CHAPTER 8

The next week, the school receives its first load of wood for the winter. As Grant's students saw and chop the wood, Grant recalls his own elementary school days and his teacher Matthew Antoine. A bitter, defeated man, Mr. Antoine hated teaching and hated his students. Grant calls Mr. Antoine a mulatto, referring to Antoine's mixed race. Because he was a mulatto, Mr. Antoine considered himself superior to blacks and felt contempt for black people who wished to learn in a society that thinks them subhuman. After Grant studied at a university for several years, he returned to the plantation to teach in the school. He went to visit Mr. Antoine, who advised Grant to do his best but did not think Grant could help the situation. According to Mr. Antoine, blacks had but one option in the South: to run away.

ANALYSIS: CHAPTERS 6–8

In these chapters, Gaines illustrates the racism that plagues Grant. Sheriff Guidry agrees to let Grant visit Jefferson, but in warning Grant against aggravating Jefferson, Guidry denies Grant the right to elicit an emotional response from Jefferson. Guidry wishes Jefferson to remain meek and without convictions. Grant's school operates at the mercy of the racist white community, receiving basic supplies like chalk, books, and firewood at the whim of the whites. Dr. Joseph sees the black children as physical laborers and implies blacks should be working in the fields as they did when they were slaves. He compliments Grant's class by calling it a "good crop"— racist language that suggests Dr. Joseph thinks of the students as objects, not people. Dr. Joseph insists on the importance of hygiene, but Grant notes the poor health of whites; Edna drinks, a fat man grunts like a hog, and Dr. Joseph himself, who insists upon physical exercise for the black children, is so fat he can hardly get into his car.

While he notes the blatant examples of white racism, Gaines also delves into the murky areas where stereotypes begin to dissolve. While Grant despises Dr. Joseph for believing that black children should grow up to work on white plantations, Grant observes that the two men who bring the wood to the school truly enjoy themselves while performing their work. He also sees how much the children enjoy physical labor, chopping and sawing the wood. He gets frustrated when he watches them, and he wonders, "Am I reaching them at all? They are acting exactly as the old men . . . who never attended school a day in their lives. Is it just a vicious circle?" He worries that blacks are so used to their chains, they have come to like them. Going along with the whites is easier than fighting them, and the children's enjoyment of the physical work makes compliance still easier.

Gaines suggests that racism is particularly difficult to root out when it comes cloaked in kindness. Edna Guidry feels empathy and goodwill for Grant, but she treats him as her inferior. She asks him questions but answers them herself. She makes observations about his life and the lives of his friends without letting him make his own observations. Edna acts out the role that she *learned* to play. Moreover, in emphasizing Edna's reliance upon bourbon, Gaines implies that alcohol plays a part in preventing Edna from truly showing compassion for Grant, or other black people, for that matter. Alcohol also plays a role in Grant's inability to change.

Professor Antoine, for all his cynical condemnation of whites, plays a role in propagating racism. Since he has white blood, he feels superior to black people, and he stayed in the South because he enjoyed this feeling of superiority. Antoine says mulattoes hate blacks because mulattoes know whites have the most financial and social worth and want to associate themselves with whites. The more white blood in a person, the higher he stands on the rungs of the social ladder. In order to deny their blackness, Antoine says, mulattoes avoid working with blacks. Antoine's is a self-hating ethos.

Grant's inner conflict stems from his experiences in education, including his exposure to the cynical Antoine. Inspired by years of study, Grant wants to make great changes in his hometown. Grant's behavior defies stereotype, but in order to live, he must follow certain rules that make his small moments of defiance futile. The losing battle between small rebellions and survival becomes clear in Grant's conversation with Guidry. Grant takes pride in flouting Guidry's racist expectations by using grammatical English and maintaining his poise, but then he feels he has been "too clever" and adopts a humble demeanor. Like the nameless black narrator in Ralph Ellison's *Invisible Man*, Grant, no matter how much he asserts himself, can control only the superficialities of his life. He can use grammatical English and get an education, but the wrath of society would descend on him if he did something truly to step out of line.

CHAPTERS 9–12

SUMMARY: CHAPTER 9

Grant takes Miss Emma to the jail in Bayonne. When they arrive, they meet two deputies, Clark and Paul. Clark orders Paul to search through the package Emma has brought for Jefferson. After a thorough inspection, they allow Emma and Grant into Jefferson's cell. They find Jefferson lying flat on his bunk, staring at the ceiling. Jefferson does not respond to Emma's questions. He refuses her food too, merely saying, "It don't matter." She asks him to clarify, and he tells her, "Nothing don't matter." In a vague manner, he asks when they are going to execute him. Emma does not understand his question, but Grant does. Emma continues to talk, but she cannot get him to say much else.

SUMMARY: CHAPTER 10
The next two visits follow a similar pattern. On the day of the fourth visit, Tante Lou tells Grant that Miss Emma is ill and cannot go to the prison today. Grant enters the house to find Miss Emma in her chair, coughing unconvincingly. Grant thinks she is feigning illness because she and his aunt expect him to go to the jail alone from now on. Grant is angry and tells them he feels humiliated performing the duties they ask of him. Through her tears, Miss Emma apologizes for humiliating him, but says she has no one else to whom she can turn for help. Grant departs.

SUMMARY: CHAPTER 11
When Grant gets to Jefferson's cell, he is unsure of what to say. He asks Jefferson if he is hungry. Jefferson asks if Grant has brought any corn, saying that hogs eat corn. Grinning angrily, Jefferson acts like a hog, kneeling down and sticking his head in the bag of food Grant brought. Grant watches him carefully and asks if Jefferson is trying to make him feel guilty so that Grant will leave him alone. He says white men think Jefferson's situation is hopeless. Jefferson does not respond. Grant wants to ask Jefferson what he is thinking about, but he stifles the impulse.

SUMMARY: CHAPTER 12
Grant knows he will have to lie to protect Miss Emma from the news of Jefferson's disturbing anger, but he cannot face her. He drives to the Rainbow Club. Sitting at the bar, he listens to some old men talking about Jackie Robinson and remembers the excitement and pride the town felt when the boxer Joe Louis achieved heroic success. He recalls a recurring dream he used to have in which a young man on his way to the electric chair cried out for Joe Louis to save him. He wonders if Jefferson would call out to Jackie Robinson for help.

Grant quickly leaves the bar and walks to the school where Vivian teaches the sixth and seventh grades. Grant finds Vivian working quietly at her desk. He asks her to leave town with him that night, but she reminds him that they should not be seen together. She does not want to give her husband any excuse to take her children. He tells her about his visit to Jefferson's cell and, once again, he tells her he wants to leave the South forever. She says he cannot bring himself to leave because he loves his people more than he hates the South. Grant says that he wants more than he has. Before they leave to get a drink, Vivian tells him that most of the teachers and students at her school know about their love affair.

ANALYSIS: CHAPTERS 9–12

Grant and Jefferson view each other as foes. During Grant's first solo visit to Jefferson's cell, Jefferson shows that he took offense at his lawyer's words, but in the absence of a true enemy to rage against, he takes out his anger on Grant. Jefferson makes it clear that being called a hog angers him more than the death sentence does. Sheriff Guidry says Jefferson can die like a "contented hog," but Jefferson is not contented, animalistic, or stupid; he realizes that his lawyer's words denied him his humanity, his will, and his spirit. Like Jefferson, Grant feels trapped and humiliated. He bemoans having to visit Jefferson, particularly if he has to go alone. Although Grant does not show the same amount of aggression that Jefferson does in the cell, Grant's will to abandon Jefferson and the South can itself be seen as an aggressive affront. Grant's inability to see the good that might come from his visits with Jefferson prevents him from interacting positively with Jefferson. Instead of calmly dealing with Jefferson's outburst, Grant reacts in an accusatory and almost petty fashion, asking Jefferson if he is trying to make him feel guilty.

Grant's discussion of Joe Louis and Jackie Robinson suggests that because few black public figures and heroes existed in the 1940s, sports figures like Joe Louis and Jackie Robinson shouldered the burden of personifying black greatness in public. These giants take on almost godlike qualities in the public eye; Grant dreams that the men could rescue the downtrodden from death. In his dream, a young man calls for Joe Louis to save him as if asking Jesus Christ for salvation. In this novel, however, Gaines shows how Jefferson and Grant come to serve as heroes for each other. Each develops a strong sense of humanity and character by working with the person in front of him, not by searching for a god to save him. Gaines does not wish to diminish the accomplishments of heroes like Joe Louis or Jackie Robinson, nor does he aim to degrade people for looking up to these heroes. Rather, he tries to show how two ordinary black men living in the troubled South become heroic figures for each other and for others too.

For Grant, Vivian and the Club both provide an escape and demand conscientiousness. While at the Club, Grant wonders whether Jefferson would ask for salvation from Jackie Robinson like the young man in his dream. In realizing that Jefferson would have to appeal to Jackie Robinson, Grant realizes that Jefferson lacks a positive role model, a hero, or a God who can actually save him. Vivian acts as Grant's conscience, drawing attention to his tendency to deny reality. After Grant expresses a longing to leave the South, Vivian brings him back to earth, saying that both she and Grant must remain in the South. She says the South is all they have, implying that despite the difficulties they face, they have an obligation to the black quarter and its inhabitants—they cannot forsake their roots and community. Vivian knows why Grant never acts upon his urge to leave the South and spells it out for him, saying, "You love them more than you hate this place." Grant says he wants more, which points both to his laudable desire to create a better life for himself and his bullheaded resistance to Vivian's sensible observations. Although with his departure and return Grant has proven Vivian right in her idea that he loves his people more he hates the South, he remains convinced that by running away he and Vivian will solve all of their problems.

Vivian is proud of her love for Grant, and, despite her will to remain in Bayonne to keep her children, she cannot hide this love. The fact that the whole school is suspicious of their relationship, and that Vivian proudly accepts and announces that they suspect it, indicates that she foresees their ultimate union with one another. Her comment here at the end of Chapter 12 shows that she enjoys the thought of living with Grant in the South. Gaines shows Vivian's emotional state here in order to heighten the ensuing clash between her and Grant that occurs later in the novel.

CHAPTERS 13–15

SUMMARY: CHAPTER 13
Miss Emma goes to church on Determination Sunday—when church members sing their favorite hymns and tell the congregation where they will spend eternity. Grant recalls last Friday, when he came back from talking to Vivian. He had found Miss Emma and Reverend Ambrose sitting with his aunt in the kitchen. Miss Emma asked him about his visit to Jefferson's cell, and he lied and says that Jefferson seemed to be doing well and that he had eaten some of the food she had sent him. Reverend Ambrose tried to determine whether or not Grant intended to teach Jefferson within a Christian framework. Reverend Ambrose had visited Jefferson and he wanted to know if Grant had been undermining his teachings with cynical

secularism. Grant became impatient with this line of questioning. After years of hard studying in academia, he no longer believes in the teachings of the Bible.

After his aunt returns from church, Grant sits at his desk correcting papers. He remarks that, up until his last year at the university, he participated in the church. He says that studying ate up most of his time and that he became distanced from his faith in the church, angering Tante Lou. Professor Antoine told him he should leave Bayonne for good, and Grant tried visiting his parents in California. Nevertheless, he returned to Bayonne to teach, where he cannot escape the influence of the black church. He says that he is "running in place, unable to accept what used to be my life, unable to leave it."

Suddenly, Vivian surprises Grant with a visit to his house.

SUMMARY: CHAPTER 14
Vivian has never been to Grant's house before. He gives her a small tour and offers her some coffee and cake. She insists they wash their plates after eating, even though Grant tells her that his aunt would take care of the dishes. He asks her to take a walk with him, and she consents. They walk through the plantation, past a cemetery, and onto the sugarcane fields. They make love on the field, concealed by the cane. Afterward, they discuss possible names for their future children, and Grant says he does not want to raise his children in this community.

SUMMARY: CHAPTER 15
After some time, they return home. Vivian says that she hopes Grant's family will like her. She comes from a light-skinned mulatto community called Free LaCove, but she married a very dark-skinned man whom she met while attending Xavier University. She kept the marriage secret because she knew her family would object. When she finally told them, they shunned her and her new family. Even now, after her separation from her husband, she never speaks to her family.

They find Tante Lou, Miss Emma, and others at his aunt's house. Grant introduces Vivian. He insists on making coffee because he and Vivian drank it all earlier, but his aunt objects, wishing to take charge in her own home. The tension between them makes the other ladies uncomfortable. Tante Lou asks Vivian about her background and beliefs. Vivian goes to church regularly, although it's to the Catholic church. Tante Lou presses Vivian about whether she would drop her religion to marry Grant, the atheist. Vivian says she hopes she would not have to do that, but that if she had to, she would. Grant quickly ushers Vivian onto the porch. Vivian tells Grant that she is happy to know that at least other families criticize their children as much as her family does. Grant insists that his family differs from hers. Vivian becomes very quiet and then says she must go. The ladies say that Vivian is a "lady of quality" and encourage her to remain a Christian woman. After the interrogation, Vivian leaves gratefully with Grant. They watch a black girl and her boyfriend walking home from church holding hands. Grant thinks to himself, "Good luck."

ANALYSIS: CHAPTERS 13–15

Despite their love for one another, Grant continues to neglect Vivian. When they stand on the porch after the initial barrage of questions from Tante Lou, Grant shows that he lacks sensitivity when he tells Vivian that he considers his family's reaction "far from being the same thing" as the situation between her family and her husband. He may not intend to hurt her, but her silence and her hasty exit indicates that she takes offense to Grant's remark. At this point, she doesn't need to feel like an outsider. She needs comfort. Recognizing the similarities between their families provides her with some comfort, but Grant proves insensitive to her feelings by contradicting her. Moreover, Grant never interacts with her children and refers to them only as "the babies," and only when they interfere with his weekend plans. He never even mentions their names to the reader, despite the fact that he and Vivian discuss the names for their future children. Though he loves Vivian, he does not recognize the fact that her children have grown up in the community. Instead, he plans to leave Louisiana one day, and he wants her to leave everything behind and go with him.

Given Grant's blindness, and given the fact that Grant's thoughts and actions represent the only point of view in the novel, the reader receives a limited picture of Vivian. Like most of the other characters in this novel, she seems to have very little significance beyond her direct influence upon Grant's daily life. This limitation reveals yet again just how harshly we must criticize Grant and question how he relates information. We perceive characters and events through the eyes of a single, biased narrator. Even so, Gaines provides glimpses of Vivian's character— her strength and resolve, her critical and sensitive nature—when he shows how she reacts critically to Grant both in these chapters and in their previous conversations.

Ultimately, Vivian will confront Grant and burst his self-indulgent bubble, further displaying her vivid and powerful emotional life.

Vivian's family illustrates how mulattoes displayed prejudice toward blacks, but Grant and Tante Lou illustrate how African-Americans of strict African heritage often act distrustfully toward mulattoes as well, even well-meaning people like Vivian. The ladies description of Vivian as a "lady of quality" includes elements of both praise and a mild resentment. Tante Lou says, "quality ain't cheap," degrading Vivian as an object for sale even while she puts her on a pedestal. Grant himself shows his resentment toward mulattoes when he tells Vivian that his family is "far from being the same thing" as hers. Both Grant and Tante Lou allow their defensive stance to affect negatively their relationships with well-meaning mulattoes. Recalling his description of the bitter Professor Antoine from Chapter 8, Gaines again addresses the paradoxical relationship between blacks and mulattoes, showing how racism breeds divisiveness within the African-American community itself.

Grant indicates that his conflict with the church stems more from his inner conflict with himself than from a serious critique of the church. Gaines does not clarify in the novel whether Grant truly believes in a higher power called "God," but he clearly indicates that Grant has little patience for any of the traditional church practices in which his aunt finds comfort. As we will later discover, Grant believes that the Christian church merely functions to keep black people in a subservient state, and that the God worshipped by his family and friends, therefore, is nothing more than a white God. However, Grant's statement about "running in place" indicates that something inside prevents him from fully extracting himself from his community and his church. He feels drawn to his place of birth while simultaneously wishing to run away, indicating that he understands to a certain extent that his hard-and-fast interpretation of the black church as a white tool lacks sophistication. Having distanced himself from his community while at the university, Grant cannot see the positive values associated with the church.

CHAPTERS 16–18

SUMMARY: CHAPTER 16

On Monday, Grant sees Tante Lou, Reverend Ambrose, and Miss Emma returning from visiting Jefferson. They stop at Miss Emma's house and go inside. In school, Grant finds his students planning for the annual Christmas program. He reminds them to keep just one person in mind this Christmas season, referring to Jefferson.

At her request, Grant visits Miss Emma. Miss Emma knows Grant lied about his previous visit to Jefferson, because her own visit was disturbing: Jefferson asked her if she had any "corn for a hog," asking viciously and repeatedly until Miss Emma grew so distressed that she slapped him. Grant is irritated, feeling once again that he cannot help Jefferson and stating that he will not let Jefferson make him feel guilty. Tante Lou insists that Grant continue his visits.

Summary: Chapter 17

Over the course of the week, Grant feels his anger dissipating. He reflects on the fact that he never stays angry for a long time, although he never believes in anything for very long either.

On Friday, when Grant enters Jefferson's cell, he has no idea how to help Jefferson. He tries talking about Miss Emma and the pain Jefferson causes her. Jefferson says that Grant wouldn't be talking about love and compassion if Grant sat on death row. Jefferson says he never asked to be born. Saying that Grant's visits anger him, Jefferson threatens to scream and cause a ruckus. Grant thinks that despite Jefferson's angry words, his eyes indicate that he needs Grant. Jefferson says only the living need to have good manners; then he throws his food on the floor.

At Guidry's request, Grant enters his office and stands for a few minutes, waiting as the sheriff talks on the phone. When Guidry finally hangs up, he asks Grant whether or not he sees an improvement in Jefferson, and Grant answers sincerely that he does not. Guidry is angry, and Grant finds out later that his anger stems from a visit Miss Emma paid to Mrs. Guidry, during which she asked if she could meet with Jefferson in the dayroom or in some other large room so that she could sit down. Grant denies Guidry's accusation that Grant encouraged Miss Emma to make the request. Guidry asks Clark and a "fat man" named Frank what he should do. Clark declares that Jefferson should remain in his cell, Frank declines to answer, and Guidry decides to ask Jefferson what he would prefer. Still, Guidry says, even if Jefferson gets to go to the dayroom, he will have to be in shackles.

Summary: Chapter 18

As promised, Guidry asks Jefferson if he would like to meet his visitors in the dayroom, and he says he would. When Miss Emma, Tante Lou, and Reverend Ambrose visit Jefferson in the day room,

Jefferson's arms and legs are shackled. He sits down at the table and Miss Emma tries to feed him, but he refuses to eat.

Grant goes to visit Jefferson. Again, Jefferson refuses to eat. Grant mentions the Christmas program, and Jefferson asks whether Christmas was when Christ was born or when he died. Grant responds, "Born." Jefferson says that Easter was when "they nailed Him to the cross." Grant asks Jefferson if he knows what "moral" means. He reminds Jefferson that human beings have an obligation to each other. Jefferson insists that he is only a hog, not a human being.

ANALYSIS: CHAPTERS 16–18

Grant begins to realize that he has a capricious nature. His anger waxes and wanes, and his beliefs shift quickly. Sometimes he agrees with Professor Antoine's cynical worldview, sometimes he feels more optimistic than his teacher. Grant alternates between neutrality and near-desperation, between insisting he cannot help Jefferson and determining to reach Jefferson somehow. First, he complains to Miss Emma that he does not want to go back to Jefferson; he then tries to engage Jefferson positively when he visits him. Gaines shows how Grant begins to sense his own failings, and, in doing so, he begins to enable himself to evoke positive change in Jefferson. This change is not immediately perceptible, but even though Jefferson continues to shun his food and to sarcastically and aggressively insist that he is a hog, at least Grant begins to find some strength in these scenes.

Sheriff Guidry both embodies and defies the characteristics of the typically racist white man. Gaines's description shows that Grant and the other black characters would face harsh consequences for displaying insolence or disrespect toward Guidry and other men of his ilk. Grant must stand and wait while the sheriff uses the phone, and he must end each sentence by calling Guidry "sir." However, at times Guidry transcends the stereotypical behavior of the bigoted, authoritarian, white racist. Even though Grant's visits to Jefferson have become a nuisance, Guidry cannot bring himself to end the visitation rights. He also makes a concession to Miss Emma, even though she went behind his back to ask his wife about meeting Jefferson in the dayroom. Gaines juxtaposes Guidry's softening heart with the unfeeling reactions of the other whites in the room. Whereas Chuck has no pity for the black man, and Frank refuses to consider his plight, Guidry displays gruff feeling for Jefferson. Guidry tries to maintain his authority while granting concessions not only to his wife, but to Miss Emma, Jefferson, and possibly his own conscience.

By refusing to use his intellectual and spiritual capabilities, Jefferson becomes the negative archetype of his race. He decides to carry the mantle of inferiority placed on him, rather than fight to shake it off. From perversity and anger, he willingly embodies all of the stereotypes whites heap on blacks: he does not think or act independently; he does not fight against his oppressors; he is more animal than man. By embodying these stereotypes and acting like an animal, he throws the ugliness of stereotypes in the face of his black friends and relations. Although Jefferson insists he does not want Grant's help, he undermines that assertion by showing Grant how much his lawyer's humiliating words hurt him. When he roots about in his food and calls himself a hog, he wordlessly shows Grant his anger and shame at being called a hog, and asks Grant for help in digging himself out of the stereotype he has come to embody. For the first half of this novel, Jefferson is not only physically imprisoned, he is spiritually imprisoned by his own unhappiness.

CHAPTERS 19–21

SUMMARY: CHAPTER 19

The community has located a pine tree and raised enough money to buy clothes for Jefferson. Grant's class puts on a Christmas program and Reverend Ambrose delivers the introductory prayer, commenting on the foolishness of those who believe themselves educated when they have no love for the Lord. Grant contains his irritation. During the Christmas program, a particularly dramatic recitation of "'Twas the Night before Christmas" affects everyone deeply, but Grant becomes depressed thinking about the monotony of their routine. Every year they put on the same play and sing the same songs. He wonders whether anything will ever change in his town. A young child brings Grant some food, and he sits looking at the gift intended for Jefferson.

SUMMARY: CHAPTER 20

The date of Jefferson's execution has been set, and Grant goes to Henri Pichot's house. Reverend Ambrose has already arrived at Pichot's, but Sheriff Guidry has not. The housekeeper assures Grant that Guidry is "on his way," but Grant is dubious. After a few minutes, however, Guidry arrives. Guidry informs the others that Jefferson will die between noon and three on the second Friday after Easter. The Mayor did not want the execution to be any closer to Easter or during Lent. Grant bitterly thinks about the fact that twelve white men convicted Jefferson and now a white man has set the date of his death. He wonders how any man could set the date of another's death and questions whether this procedure deserves to be called justice.

SUMMARY: CHAPTER 21

Grant visits Miss Emma, who lies under a quilt on her bed, looking extremely ill. Grant badly wants to leave, but he knows he should spend at least a few minutes there. After ten minutes, he returns to his aunt's house where Vivian pays him a visit. Vivian says she wants to stop by Miss Emma's but does not know whether it is a good time. Grant tells Vivian he wants her to be part of his life and that his aunt will have to accept that. They get out of bed and go to Miss Emma's. Vivian whispers something into Miss Emma's ear and Emma looks pleased.

At the Rainbow Club, Grant and Vivian drink brandy, and he tells her why he thinks his aunt and Miss Emma ask so much of him. He says they want to take pride in him, just as Miss Emma wants to take pride in Jefferson. Vivian has put down her glass and says she does not understand. Grant says black men have historically failed to protect their women—either staying in the South and losing their will, or running away and leaving the women to look after the children. Grant insists that even those who try to change things will break because they must shoulder the burdens of all those who have failed before them. It is a vicious circle. Miss Emma and Tante Lou cling to Grant, he says, because they see that he is different from other men. They do not understand, however, that by holding on to him they force him to shoulder a terrible burden and facilitate his destruction. When Vivian asks how they can break the circle, Grant replies, "It's up to Jefferson, my love."

ANALYSIS: CHAPTERS 19–21

Although Grant wants to help his community, he feels powerless to do so. This feeling of powerlessness makes him bitter. At the Christmas program, he reflects that nothing changes: not the songs, not the clothes, not the people. Grant feels he cannot help or change these people, and in order to stop this failure from hurting him, he nurtures anger and contempt toward the people he says he wants to help. He fans the flames of his superiority and separates himself from the happiness of the group. Still, despite his best efforts to be callous, Grant notices sights and moments that depress him with their tenderness: a girl in his class gives a lovely and affecting reading of "'Twas the Night before Christmas"; a present for Jefferson sits against the pathetic Christmas tree, a present the children bought with their own contributions of nickels and dimes; a plate of food brought to Grant by a child who has noticed his misery.

Reverend Ambrose's introductory prayer challenges Grant to show true faith. The reverend thinks that when you believe in God, you not only comfort yourself, you take a step toward fighting the injustice of a white-dominated society. God is a source of hope, change, and rebellion. Moreover, if you have faith in God, you have faith in your people. Nevertheless, Grant is not up to that challenge, at least not yet. Reverend Ambrose's sermon is a precursor for his diatribe against Grant in a later chapter.

One can interpret Grant's statement, that Jefferson can play a powerful role in breaking the cycle of black men's failures, in numerous ways. The statement might illustrate Grant's new humility, as he shows that Jefferson, not Grant, will be the real hero for black men. At the same time, the statement might indicate Grant's renewed belief in his own task—namely, the task of helping Jefferson regain his humanity. But one might also interpret the statement more cynically, as an indicator of Grant's continued bitterness. By laying responsibility at Jefferson's feet, Grant might be admitting that he himself cannot play the role of savior for the community. Or, Grant might be shirking his duties by saying the choice is Jefferson's— if Grant fails to transform Jefferson into a dignified man, he will not have to take the blame. The numerous possible interpretations point to the complexity of Grant's character. We already know that he often acts like both a cynic and a saint; it is certainly possible that he has both selfish and unselfish reasons for making this statement.

Gaines associates Christian imagery with Jefferson: like Christ, Jefferson has been unjustly sentenced to death by a society that fears and hates him. Also like Christ, Jefferson represents the potential for human change, and the manner in which he goes to his death will do either great harm or great good to the community. In the bar, Grant refers to Jefferson as a savior. Jefferson himself seems to sense the association, asking several times about Christ's death. When the governor sets the execution date, he avoids Easter Sunday perhaps because he wishes to avoid associating Jefferson with Christ, and making a martyr of him. Because the governor pays attention to the symbolism of Easter Sunday, he gives the symbolism more weight and importance.

CHAPTERS 22–24

SUMMARY: CHAPTER 22

> *I want me a whole gallona ice cream.*
> *(See* QUOTATIONS, *p. 55)*

Grant goes to the courthouse to see Jefferson. Paul reluctantly searches the package of food for Jefferson. When Grant enters Jefferson's cell, the conversation goes much better this time. Grant asks Jefferson if he would like anything, and Jefferson responds that he would like a gallon of vanilla ice cream to make up for the rest of his life, when he never got enough ice-cream. Jefferson likes Grant's offer to bring him a little radio.

Grant borrows money from people at the Rainbow Club. He goes to a little store uptown to buy a small radio. The white sales clerk wants to give Grant the floor model instead of a brand new radio, but Grant stands his ground and the clerk caves in. Grant takes the radio to the courthouse, receives the sheriff's permission to give it to Jefferson, and gives the radio to Paul to deliver to Jefferson.

SUMMARY: CHAPTER 23

When Miss Emma, Tante Lou, and Reverend Ambrose go to see Jefferson, they have to visit him in his cell because Jefferson refuses to leave his radio. They find him lying down on his bunk, staring at the wall and listening to music. He does not say a word. When they return home, Tante Lou blames Grant for the problem. Reverend Ambrose says that the radio is a sinful influence on Jefferson. Grant becomes furious. Last Friday was the first time Jefferson had ever opened up to him, and Grant refuses to take the radio away from Jefferson and potentially undo whatever progress he has made.

Grant goes back to see Jefferson. He brings a big bag of nuts that his students gathered for Jefferson. When Grant asks Jefferson to meet Miss Emma in the dayroom next time, Jefferson consents. Grant offers to bring Jefferson a little notebook so that he can write down any thoughts that come to his mind, and Jefferson agrees to the plan. As Grant leaves, Jefferson asks him with some hesitation to thank the children for the nuts. Grant is overjoyed, and he feels as if

he has found religion. Stifling his impulse to hug Jefferson, Grant
squeezes Jefferson's hand kindly and leaves.

SUMMARY: CHAPTER 24

> *I want you to show them the difference between what
> they think you are and what you can be.*
>   *(See* QUOTATIONS, *p. 56)*

Grant joins Miss Emma on her next visit to Jefferson, bringing along
a notebook and pencil. In the dayroom, Jefferson refuses to eat at
first. Grant asks Jefferson to walk with him around the room. As
they walk, Grant tells Jefferson that a hero does something other
men do not do or cannot do. Grant says that he (Grant) is not a hero,
but that Jefferson can be a hero. Grant tells Jefferson about the
white myth that black people are not human. Grant says he cannot
stand up to defy whites, and that the reverend will not stand up to
defy them, but Jefferson can do it. Grant tells Jefferson that he needs
him more than Jefferson needs Grant. As Grant speaks, Jefferson
cries quietly at his side, and Grant begins to cry too.

ANALYSIS: CHAPTERS 22–24

Grant's experience in the department store shows how a racist society is racist even in its smallest interactions. Black citizens must
depend on the caprices of whites, and if whites, such as the saleswoman who waits on Grant, do not feel like being fair, black people
have no recourse. Although black people are no longer physically
enslaved, in many ways, they are spiritually enslaved. Grant's
refusal to bow down to the saleswoman's shoddy treatment represents a victory for him. He insists that she give him a new radio, and
in the end she agrees. This turn of events does not seem like an
immense victory, but it is an important one. Gaines suggests that the
cunning evil of racism is the way it pervades daily life and begins to
seem normal. Tiny moments that make black people feel second-
class add up to total oppression. Refusing to tolerate even minor
shoddy treatment makes a difference.

In these chapters, Jefferson begins to take steps toward recover-
ing his dignity by voicing and acting upon personal desires. He
admits to Grant that he wants ice cream and consents to write his
thoughts down in a notebook. A few days later, he asks Grant to
thank his students for their efforts. These may seem like minor incidents, but they mark the end of Jefferson's isolation. Until this point,

he has refused to admit wanting anything. Since acknowledging his intelligent desires is a human action, Jefferson seems to be relinquishing his tendency to deny his humanity. Now he reclaims his humanity by admitting he wants things and by thinking of others' feelings. The fact that Jefferson weeps following Grant's eloquent appeal for Jefferson's heroic strength shows that he has begun to listen to and internalize Grant's thoughts and feelings.

Both Grant and Jefferson go through pivotal changes as they walk around the room. In contrast to his previous wild behavior, now Jefferson listens carefully to Grant's words, looking up when asked to do so. He weeps as Grant talks, showing that Grant's words have affected him. In contrast to Grant's usual cynicism, depression, and disconnectedness, here he talks in emotional and straightforward language. To Jefferson, he speaks the raw emotions of his heart as he never speaks them to other people. He tells Jefferson of his own shame, his own failings, his own need for a hero. He admits he has always wanted to run from responsibility and has squandered his chance to make changes. He stops expressing anger at his family and fellow black community members and starts expressing anger at his society. Grant's honesty and his inspiring words begin to convince Jefferson that he can stop acting like an animal and regain his dignity. If Jefferson and Grant have clashed in the past, now they become united in working toward one goal. Gaines stresses this unification with the image of the two men walking together.

CHAPTERS 25–28

SUMMARY: CHAPTER 25
Grant cannot find Vivian at the Rainbow Club. He sits at the bar and orders a drink. In a corner behind him, two mulatto bricklayers talk loudly, hoping Grant will overhear them. Grant finally catches a few of their words. They state loudly that Jefferson should have been executed long ago. Grant tries to contain himself, but after a few minutes he loses control. He walks over and tells them to be quiet. A fight breaks out, during which Grant is knocked unconscious.

SUMMARY: CHAPTER 26
When Grant wakes up, he finds himself in Vivian's bedroom. He discovers that Claiborne, unable to stop the fight, knocked him out, and that Vivian brought him here to recover. Despite her disapproval of violence, Vivian softens and asks Grant to stay the night.

He knows that he should not, since her husband could return to try to get the children. She tells Grant that she needs more from him than he currently gives her, that she wants more consideration. Angry, he walks out of the room and stands at the front door. He looks out through the screen and into the darkness. He does not want to go outside, for he realizes that everything he cares for is in Vivian's house. After a few minutes, he returns to the kitchen and buries his face in Vivian's lap.

SUMMARY: CHAPTER 27
Reverend Ambrose talks to Grant about Jefferson. He wants Grant to help him teach Jefferson about God, but Grant no longer believes in the church and refuses to help the reverend. Reverend Ambrose gets angry and raises his voice to Grant, calling him "boy" and telling him that he is uneducated because he does not know or understand people. Grant says he cannot lie to Jefferson by pretending to believe in heaven or the Bible. Reverend Ambrose says he knows Grant looks down on him for lying, and he admits that he does lie in order to relieve people's pain, but he says that people lie to themselves and to others in order to make life bearable. He tells Grant that Tante Lou has been lying to him all her life, telling herself and Grant she was fine when truly she was working her fingers to the bone in order to send him to college.

SUMMARY: CHAPTER 28
When Grant next goes to visit Jefferson, he sees the notebook on the floor, next to the radio. He opens the notebook and finds that Jefferson has filled up three-quarters of the first page, though he clearly erased a great deal. He has written about dying, and about the difference between men and hogs. Grant asks him about Reverend Ambrose's last visit. Jefferson says Ambrose told him to pray, but that he does not pray because he doesn't know if heaven exists. Jefferson asks Grant if he prays and Grant replies honestly, saying he doesn't because he doesn't believe in anything. Grant says he feels lost. He tells Jefferson that he wants Jefferson to believe in something so that someday Grant can look to Jefferson as an example and start believing in something himself.

Jefferson says that Reverend Ambrose told him to give up his possessions, which confuses Jefferson because he has so few possessions to give up. Grant says Jefferson may not have possessions, but he still has love to give. Jefferson says that everyone asks him to bear a cross, but no one ever bore his cross. Jefferson asks if Miss Emma or even Grant would go to the chair to save him. When Jefferson asks if Grant believes in God, Grant says he does. Jefferson says he wants to go to his death wordlessly, as Christ did. He talks of his execution, saying Grant asks too much of him. Jefferson says that he moved through his life working and grinning to get by, pandering to the whites, doing what he thought God asked of him, and now the people around him want him to change entirely. When Grant lowers his head, Jefferson accuses him of not being able to look at him. Grant looks, and sees Jefferson standing tall, not stooped. Jefferson asks Grant how the execution will feel. Grant continues to avert his gaze from Jefferson, but accepts a sweet potato when Jefferson offers it.

ANALYSIS: CHAPTERS 25–28

In these chapters, Grant becomes not teacher but student. Grant is lost and needs Jefferson's help, as he admits to Jefferson. Grant also admits to the reverend that he is lost. Reverend Ambrose says he himself is found, for he understands that the black community needs the church in order to bear life in the racist South. Ambrose also says that lying is necessary in order to make life endurable and to help others, like Grant, make progress in the world. Here Ambrose changes his tactics slightly. Before, he challenged Grant solely on religious grounds, insulting him as a secular teacher. Now he talks not just about faith in God, but about kindness to friends and family. This argument seems to reach Grant. In addressing these subjects, Ambrose highlights the absurdity facing the black community—namely, the fact that the community must continually compromise its own sense of ethical behavior—honesty—in order to survive in an unethical and racist world. Ambrose's emphasis on lying attracts Grant because he too has had to lie in the past—for instance, when he lied to Miss Emma about Jefferson's aggression. Grant can identify with Ambrose's words here and even puts them into practice. When he speaks to Jefferson in Chapter 28, Grant tries to persuade him to believe in religion whether Jefferson believes it will be good for his soul or not.

Jefferson begins teaching Grant to stop wallowing in his own pain and fear. Whereas Jefferson once lay mute on his bed and refused to talk, now he continually confronts Grant, demanding to know whether Grant has faith in heaven and God, and whether the people who want Jefferson to die for them would die for Jefferson. Grant has difficulty answering these questions and lowers his head in shame because he cannot bear to look at Jefferson. Jefferson confronts

Grant about this reaction too, telling him that he should look at him. Jefferson's posture marks his change: he stands up straight now. Jefferson's relationship to food shows the change too; before he refused to eat when others offered him food, but now he offers food to Grant. He acts as Grant should act, lifting his head up and being brave.

Vivian also teaches Grant, showing him that he lacks consideration for other people and that his cynicism conveniently allows him to isolate himself and avoid dealing with other people's pain. Grant claims to love Vivian, but he focuses attention on his own life, not on hers. He thinks of her not as a person with needs of her own, but as his distraction, his means of obtaining comfort, and his haven in times of distress. Vivian's personal life is merely a nuisance to Grant, a source of complications and obstacles. Vivian seldom speaks in the novel—which reflects Grant's minimal interest in her—but here she asserts herself and breaks into Grant's world. Grant tells her, "That's not you talking, honey," as if he understands her better than she does herself. Vivian replies, "Who *is* me?" in order to emphasize the fact that Grant does not truly know her. She forces him to decide whether or not he wants to pay real attention to her. By burying his head in her lap, Grant agrees to do what Vivian asks.

CHAPTER 29: JEFFERSON'S DIARY

SUMMARY

Good by mr wigin tell them im strong tell them im
a man   *(See* QUOTATIONS, *p. 57)*

This chapter consists of Jefferson's diary. Jefferson has never received much formal education, and misspellings fill the diary. Some of the time, he addresses his writing to Grant, as if writing a letter. Jefferson writes about the other men in prison and wonders why poor people seem to suffer so much more than the rich do. He concludes that the Lord caters to white people. A few days later, Jefferson writes about Grant's assertion that he is better than white people think. Jefferson wants proof of his worth. He says he has never done so much thinking in his life, and he begins to realize how little he has always expected of himself.

The Monday before Jefferson's execution, he writes that the sheriff, Mr. Pichot, and Mr. Morgan visit him in his cell. Jefferson hears Mr. Morgan and Sheriff Guidry talking about their bet. Mr. Morgan wants to double the stakes. He bets that Grant will fail. Mr.

Pichot asks Jefferson how he is doing and then offers to sharpen his pencil with his own knife. Then, with Guidry's permission, Pichot gives Jefferson the knife. Jefferson says he will give it back in a few days. During the next few days, people from all over town come to speak to Jefferson. His friend Bok reluctantly gives Jefferson one of his marbles, and Jefferson cries because no one has ever paid so much attention to him.

Vivian comes with Grant to visit Jefferson on his last night. Jefferson is humiliated in front of her, for he has not bathed recently and thinks he is ugly, but Vivian tells him he looks handsome and strong. She kisses his face. Jefferson apologizes to Grant for crying when Grant told him he would not be at the execution. He explains that he cried because nobody was ever as good to him as Grant is— nobody but Grant made him feel he is somebody.

Guidry asks what Jefferson wants for supper and Jefferson asks for his godmother's cooking and a little ice cream for dessert. After Jefferson has dinner and a shower, Guidry asks him if he feels he was treated well. Jefferson says he does, and Guidry says he should write that in his tablet. Guidry offers to leave the light on so that he can continue to write. Jefferson cannot sleep and writes in his journal. He resolves to see the sunrise on his last morning. He says he cannot listen to the radio because it plays only for the living. Jefferson is afraid, but determined to stay strong. He writes goodbye to Mr. Wiggins and asks him to "tell them im a man." He says he will give the diary to Paul to deliver to Grant.

ANALYSIS

Jefferson's diary testifies to the mutual benefits he and Grant get from their friendship and love for one another. Grant bought the diary for Jefferson, and Jefferson writes in it usually as if writing a letter to Grant. Even when he is alone in his cell, Jefferson can write to Grant and feel he has companionship. As Jefferson writes down his thoughts, he begins to think seriously about the world and his role in it. Showing the influence of Grant's words, Jefferson writes that he realizes how important he has become to his community. Moreover, the diary will serve as a boon for Grant's self-confidence and his sense of self-worth, as he himself initiated the use of the diary by engaging Jefferson and buying him the notebook and pencil.

The white characters are not uniformly cruel to Jefferson, although their token kindnesses do not matter much in the face of the death penalty their people imposed on Jefferson. Mr. Pichot shows some compassion toward Jefferson by offering to sharpen his pencil and then giving him the knife as a gift. Guidry kindly offers to leave the light on so Jefferson can write. Also, in the past, Guidry has allowed numerous visitors to see Jefferson. Guidry asks Jefferson to speak well of him in the diary, perhaps both because he wants kind things written about him and because he is anxious for Jefferson to like him.

Jefferson's diary indicates that he places his faith in his tangible friendship with Grant, not necessarily in God. Jefferson does not know whether he should put his faith in religion, since different people say different things about it. Some say heaven does not exist for blacks, but Reverend Ambrose says heaven is for all people. Jefferson's touching apology to Grant for crying shows that he worries about Grant's feelings and about what Grant thinks of him. He credits Grant for convincing him that he is somebody. His diary attests to the fact that some combination of Grant's influence and Jefferson's own strength has allowed Jefferson to face his death with almost superhuman calm and understanding.

Gaines shows that the uneducated can possess intelligence and nobility. Misspellings and grammatical errors fill Jefferson's diary, but they do nothing to detract from the sophistication of his thoughts and the bravery and sadness that comes through in his writing. In some ways, Jefferson's writing seems superior to Grant's. We know Grant's writing intimately; he narrates the novel except for this chapter. Although Grant writes intelligent, affecting prose, he does not match the unembarrassed expression of emotion that comes through in Jefferson's writing. Neither does he match Jefferson's lyricism, especially in the last few lines of the diary, in which Jefferson notes the bluebird singing and the blue sky in the last few hours before his death.

CHAPTERS 30–31

SUMMARY: CHAPTER 30
On the morning before Jefferson's execution, a black truck with a gray tarpaulin cover drives into town. Many people stop to watch it pass. It goes through the business district and pulls into the courthouse.

Vivian and Grant sit at the Rainbow Club the night before the execution. She tells him that from noon until she knows the execution is over, she will have her students kneel beside their desks. After saying goodnight to Vivian at nine o'clock, Grant drives around for a while and then goes to his aunt's house. He notices a couple of cars parked in front of Miss Emma's, but he does not stop.

At six-thirty the next morning, Sheriff Guidry sits down to breakfast, feeling nervous. He has never overseen an execution before. He tells his wife that he asked Grant if he would be present, but Grant shook his head. Guidry says Reverend Ambrose asked to attend the execution and Guidry said yes. He also asked the Reverend if one more person from the quarter would like to attend. At eight, Guidry goes to the courthouse and supervises the unloading process. Henry Vincent, the official executioner, tells the sheriff that the prisoner must be shaven. Guidry asks Paul to do it, and Paul reluctantly agrees.

Jefferson remains quiet as Paul shaves his head, ankles, and wrists. As Paul leaves, Jefferson asks him to deliver the notebook to Grant and to keep the radio for himself. Paul says he cannot keep the radio, but he promises to give it to the other inmates. He accepts Jefferson's gift of a marble. Jefferson asks Paul if he plans to attend the execution and Paul says yes.

SUMMARY: CHAPTER 31

As the hour of Jefferson's execution approaches, Grant steps outside the schoolhouse. He remembers old friends, classmates, and baseball teammates. Many of his friends have died, mostly as a result of violence. Grant stifles tears for Jefferson, saying that there will be too many more like him, and he cannot cry for all of them. He thinks of calling Vivian or the Reverend. He thinks Reverend Ambrose is courageous for using the white man's God as a source of strength. Grant wonders if he has caused Jefferson to lose faith in God and asks Jefferson to forgive his foolishness if he has robbed him of faith. Grant says he puts his faith in Jefferson.

At ten minutes before noon, Grant lines up his students and asks them to kneel. He goes back outside. He wonders what Jefferson is doing at this very minute and asks himself why he is not with Jefferson, or inside praying with his students. Angry, Grant says that he refuses to believe in the same God worshipped by the jurors that convicted Jefferson. Tante Lou, Miss Emma, and Reverend Ambrose believe in God because it frees their minds and gives their bodies a chance to be free. Grant says he knows this because "he knows what it means to be a slave. I am a slave."

At last, Paul's car approaches the church. Paul parks his car nearby and brings Jefferson's notebook to Grant. Paul says that as

Jefferson walked toward the electric chair he exuded more strength than any man in the room. He tells Grant he considers him a wonderful teacher for helping Jefferson, but Grant says that he did very little and that maybe Jefferson caused the change. Or, he says sarcastically, maybe God changed Jefferson. Paul offers Grant his hand and asks to be his friend. Grant takes the hand. When Grant goes back to his students, he faces them and cries.

ANALYSIS: CHAPTERS 30–31

Like the first chapter in the novel, Chapter 30 relates information from an undisclosed perspective, blurring our conception of reality. The chapter follows the thoughts and actions of characters besides Grant, indicating that either Grant uses his imagination in writing these sections or that Gaines temporarily uses an omniscient narrator to show us different perspectives. This shift in perspective enables Gaines to present his detailed account of Grant's individual story in the context of a greater story—the plight of his community, and even the plight of the white people in the town. The final chapters focus more and more on Grant's connection to other people. In particular, while standing outside the schoolhouse, Grant shows his connection with numerous people, both from his past and from his present. His heart yearns for Reverend Ambrose, Vivian, his baseball buddies, and Jefferson. The novel ends with Grant's noticeable connection with the white deputy, Paul. Moreover, the connection of Paul's and Grant's hands and Grant's subsequent weeping in the schoolhouse recall specific moments in Jefferson's development during Grant's visits. Gaines has already shown the pressing of hands between Jefferson and Grant and the weeping that followed Grant's eloquent speech. Here, he gives the impression that Grant too is a humble hero, connected with humanity. Finally, Grant's crying in front of his students shows that he is finally ready to connect with the children with whom his has been so strict throughout the novel. He is ready to be a leader because he is ready to be vulnerable.

Before dying, Jefferson completes his transformation into a dignified, compassionate, exemplary human being. When Paul enters the cell to shave Jefferson, he notices that Jefferson stands up immediately and that the radio has been turned off. Before, Jefferson's bunk and his radio allowed him to isolate himself. He used to lie on the bed and listen to the radio in order to block out the world. In leaving these props behind, Jefferson shows that he wishes to face reality. Of all the people involved in the execution, only Jefferson faces the event unflinchingly. He becomes even more strongly identified with Christ in these last chapters. He seems to convert Paul, who says Jefferson was the "strongest man in the room." Grant addresses his thoughts to Jefferson in the final chapter as if praying to Jesus Christ for forgiveness or assistance. Grant asks Jefferson to forgive him and says, "My faith is in you, Jefferson." For Grant, Jefferson has become a hero to emulate in times of despair.

Gaines does not impose a tidy transformation on Grant, who persists with his sarcasm, fear, and self-loathing until the last page of the novel. Although he despises himself for it, he cannot muster up the courage to attend the execution, and he cannot muster up the humility to kneel and pray with his students. He refuses to cry for Jefferson, asking himself if he wants to start weeping for all of the persecuted black men and women in the world. When Paul visits and makes heartrending overtures of sorrow and friendship, Grant hardly answers him. He expresses outrage at the whites' God, and he provokes Paul's disapproval by saying sarcastically that perhaps God helped Jefferson.

Still, much in Grant has changed. He risked emotional pain by reaching out to Jefferson. He begs Jefferson's forgiveness for possibly allowing him to lose faith in God. He grudgingly accepts Paul's overtures, agreeing to shake the proffered hand. He gives Jefferson credit for becoming strong and good. He cries at the end of the novel, allowing himself to weep for Jefferson even if it might mean he has to start weeping for all black people, and allowing himself to feel the emotion he has repressed throughout the novel.

Important Quotations Explained

1. What justice would there be to take this life? Justice,
    gentlemen? Why, I would just as soon put a hog in the
    electric chair as this.

In Chapter 1, Jefferson's defense attorney asks the jury to spare
Jefferson's life by implying it would be cruel to kill a man no more
intelligent or moral than a hog. He voices the ugly belief, held by
many whites, that blacks are animals. Jefferson becomes haunted by
the idea and begins acting like a hog, angrily refusing to talk and
rooting through his food. Miss Emma realizes the impact the attorney's words have on Jefferson and makes it her business to ensure
Jefferson dies like a man, not like an animal. When Jefferson decides
to die with dignity, he shakes off the jeering stereotypes pinned on
him by whites. Furthermore, because the attorney expressed a stereotype about blacks held by many whites, when Jefferson acts
nobly he acts on behalf of an entire oppressed community.

2.   It doesn't matter anymore. Just do the best you can. But it
     won't matter.

Matthew Antoine, Grant's primary school teacher, was a defeated,
bitter man whose attitude affected Grant's perception of Southern
society. In Chapter 8, Grant recalls visiting Antoine on his deathbed
and hearing him say these words. Grant thought he could change
things for the better through his teaching, and Antoine disagreed,
saying even Grant's best efforts would fail. Antoine's belief in black
failure has a firm basis in fact, for his society does make it nearly
impossible for blacks to succeed. However, the belief also stems
from his own racism. Antoine is of mixed race and frankly admits
that he feels superior to blacks and inferior to whites. He also admits
these notions of superiority are not natural, but created by society.
Still, he suggests that after your own inferiority gets drummed into
your head, it no longer matters if you are actually inferior or only
treated as if you are.

Grant resists Antoine's defeatism at first, but by the time the
novel begins he has come to embrace it. He believes, like Antoine,
that society forces blacks in the South to fail and that the efforts of
one man can do nothing to change things. He also begins to feel that
failure is inherent in blacks themselves, that it is not simply the effect
of an oppressive system.

3.   I want me a whole gallona ice cream.

In Chapter 22, Jefferson expresses to Grant a wish to eat vanilla ice cream. This statement marks the first step of Jefferson's recovery. Jefferson has spent the first half of this novel in a daze, asking for nothing and hardly speaking. He has expressed no personal desire, allowing people to feed him and move him around as if he is the animal his lawyer called him. With this simple desire for ice cream, he begins to act like a human again by expressing desire and personality. Jefferson's request also illustrates the beginnings of his realization of self-worth. Jefferson says he never had the opportunity to eat a filling portion of ice cream in the past. Now, for the first time, he does not wordlessly accept his meager portion, but says he would like a larger share. Although here he talks about food, this desire for more will soon spread to include a desire for more respect.

QUOTATIONS

4. I want you to show them the difference between what they think you are and what you can be.

During his visit to the jail with Miss Emma and Reverend Ambrose in Chapter 24, Grant walks with Jefferson and tells him that Jefferson's death is mightily important. Grant knows that the community will remember the execution for a long time and that Jefferson's final moments will have a powerful impact on many people. He wants to make that impact a good one, so he asks a very difficult thing of Jefferson: to die with absolute dignity. Grant wants Jefferson to show the white community that he is not an animal, as they think he is, but a dignified man, as he can be if he tries. This speech rouses the usually angry Jefferson, and he cries listening to it.

5.   Good by mr wigin tell them im strong tell them im
       a man

In Chapter 29, Jefferson writes these words to Grant in his diary.
His farewell shows he understands what his life and death mean to
his people: he wants Grant to bolster the black community by telling
them that Grant died as a strong, brave man. He addresses his last
words to the man who helped him change. Jefferson once lived a life
of unthinking submission. After the trial he lived in anger, acting out
like an animal in his cell and mistreating the people who loved him,
but now he is thoughtful and courageous. He fills his diary with ten-
der words for Grant, showing that to be a man means to reciprocate
affection. Grant also learns about reciprocating affection, from the
affection of Vivian and his family to the affection of Jefferson and
the community.

KEY FACTS

FULL TITLE
A Lesson Before Dying

AUTHOR
Ernest J. Gaines

TYPE OF WORK
Novel

GENRE
Fiction; historical fiction; social commentary

LANGUAGE
American English

DATE OF FIRST PUBLICATION
1993

PUBLISHER
Vintage Books

NARRATOR
Grant Wiggins

POINT OF VIEW
First person

TONE
Grant's narrative voice reflects his changing moods, shifting from brooding cynicism to awareness and confidence.

TENSE
Past

SETTING (TIME)
1940s

SETTING (PLACE)
Bayonne, Louisiana

PROTAGONIST
Grant Wiggins

MAJOR CONFLICT
Grant and Jefferson struggle to help Jefferson die with dignity.

RISING ACTION
Grant's regular visits to Jefferson's jail cell; Jefferson's reaction of anger and silence

CLIMAX
Grant gives a passionate speech to Jefferson, and both men cry.

FALLING ACTION
Jefferson becomes thoughtful and brave and dies an admirable death.

THEMES
Recognizing injustice and facing responsibility; redemption in death; the inescapable past

MOTIFS
Constructive lying; small displays of power; Christian imagery

SYMBOLS
The notebook; the chair; the church; food and drink

STUDY QUESTIONS & ESSAY TOPICS

STUDY QUESTIONS

1.   Why is Grant initially so reluctant to help Jefferson?

Grant's reluctance stems from his inability to confront his own fears and insecurities. Initially he tells Tante Lou that he cannot help Jefferson, implying that Jefferson is beyond hope. When Grant visits Jefferson and Jefferson behaves aggressively, Grant tells his aunt that he does not wish to proceed because he refuses to let Jefferson make him feel guilty. Although Grant is convinced that Jefferson is trying to make him feel guilty, Jefferson seems to bear no malice toward Grant in particular. Grant's unnecessary self-defense points to his subconscious conviction that he *does* bear a certain amount of the blame for Jefferson's situation, or at least for refusing to try to help Jefferson live with dignity.

Grant fears failure. When he sees Jefferson's poor mental and emotional state, he fears he might fail if he tries to help Jefferson. He also does not want to deal with Jefferson because Jefferson, by intentionally fulfilling whites' stereotypes, forces Grant to look at a physical embodiment of all the brutishness white men attribute to black men. Grant's unwillingness to act on Jefferson's behalf is part of his general unwillingness to participate in his society. He strives to keep himself separate from the unjust and oppressive world around him, and he loathes his own people because their plight depresses him. Grant knows that Jefferson's life will end because of the bigotry of a white jury, a white attorney, and a white judge. He knows that such juries exist everywhere in the country and that Jefferson grew up powerless to fight the system. He also knows that someone who realizes that such injustices exist can fight them, and that if he fails to fight them, he can be held responsible for them. In order to avoid thinking about his own complicity in the racist system, Grant initially does not want to help Jefferson.

2.   *How is Grant able to help Jefferson?*

Eventually Grant comes to believe that Jefferson can be more than a
convict, more than an oppressed black man. He comes to believe
that Jefferson can change society. Through the simple act of believing—and telling Jefferson of his belief—Grant changes Jefferson's
life. He encourages Jefferson not just to believe in himself, but also
to conceive of himself as a man more important than any man to live
in their town. Everyone, including Jefferson, always believed that
Jefferson had to learn his lowly place, but Grant teaches him that he
can define his own place. Grant helps Jefferson at first reluctantly,
and in order to succeed in teaching Jefferson how to save himself,
Grant himself must undergo a series of changes. These changes
occur during his interactions with Jefferson, but also with Vivian,
with Reverend Ambrose, and with himself. Only when Grant
changes can he help Jefferson. Only when Grant realizes and con-
fesses that he needs a savior does Jefferson become a savior.

3.   *Why do you think we never meet Vivian's children?*
     What does their absence from the novel say about Grant
     and his relationship with Vivian?

Gaines chooses the contents of the novel based on what Grant, the narrator, thinks important. We have access only to what Grant sees and hears and feels, and Grant shows very little interest in Vivian's children. He only speaks of them once, and even then he only mentions them as part of a bid to be alone with Vivian. To Grant, the children represent obstacles to his relationship with Vivian. He speaks about running away with Vivian without thinking about the effect moving would have on her children. Although Grant muses about what to name his future children, we never learn the names of Vivian's children.

The fact that Grant virtually ignores Vivian's children is only one symptom of his failure to respect her. Grant's self-centered perspective allows very little room for Vivian. He visits her only when he needs comforting and encouragement; he acts surprised when she visits him at his home. We know a few basic facts about her past, and we know that she is very beautiful. Beyond these details, however, Grant gives us very few glimpses into her life. That said, Gaines suggests Vivian's disapproval and pain in the face of Grant's inconsiderate actions. When she finally breaks down and tells Grant of her unhappiness, we are not as surprised as Grant.

QUESTIONS & ESSAYS

naîeé

4. *Why do you think Gaines chose Grant to narrate the novel? Why didn't he choose an omniscient, third-person to narrate the story?*

This novel chronicles not just Jefferson's transformation, but also Grant's transformation. By writing from Grant's point of view, Gaines emphasizes Grant's experience and transformation above the changes wrought in the other characters. Gaines could have used a third-person narrative, but Grant's telling of his own story allows us to understand the self-deceptions, the insights, and the small moments of change that mark Grant's gradual change. Also, because we likely identify with Grant more than with Jefferson, reading from Grant's perspective forces us to imagine our own reactions to the impossible situation.

QUESTIONS & ESSAYS

SUGGESTED ESSAY TOPICS

1. *Why does Reverend Ambrose call Grant uneducated?*

2. *How does Jefferson change Grant's life? How does Grant change Jefferson's life?*

3. *To what degree does Jefferson control his own transformation?*

4. *Is Jefferson a hero? Is Grant?*

5. *How does Jefferson compare to other inspirational figures in this novel (Jackie Robinson, Joe Louis, Jesus Christ)? How does Grant compare to them?*

REVIEW & RESOURCES

QUIZ

1. Where does this novel take place?

    A.   In eastern Mississippi
    B.   On a former plantation in Louisiana
    C.   In Baton Rouge
    D.   Near Gainesville, Florida

2. Why did Grant refuse to go to the trial?

    A.   He knew what the outcome would be.
    B.   He did not want to sit in the "Negroes" section.
    C.   He has never liked Jefferson.
    D.   He is spending the weekend with his girlfriend, Vivian.

3. Why does Jefferson say he took the money from the cash register?

    A.   Because he needed it and he thought no one would know
    B.   Because he forgot that Brother put it in his pocket
    C.   Because he felt he had earned it
    D.   Because he wanted to buy his nanna a present

4. What reason does Jefferson's lawyer give for sparing Jefferson's life?

    A.   He did not intend to kill anyone.
    B.   The children of the town should not have to witness an execution.
    C.   His conviction will set an unfortunate precedent.
    D.   He is no better than a fool or a hog.

5.   What is Miss Emma's relation to Jefferson?

   A.   Older sister
   B.   Godmother
   C.   Aunt
   D.   Grandmother

6.   What does Grant Wiggins teach?

   A.   High school
   B.   A remedial reading course
   C.   Math and science for adults
   D.   Primer through sixth grades

7.   Where is Grant's school located?

   A.   In the storeroom of a bar
   B.   In the church
   C.   Next to the Pichot barn
   D.   A block away from the white school

8.   What does Louis Rougon want to bet Henri Pichot when Grant visits the Pichot house for the second time?

   A.   That the execution will take place before Valentine's Day
   B.   That Grant will fail to teach Jefferson anything
   C.   That Jefferson will be found innocent on appeal
   D.   That Miss Emma will die within a month of Jefferson's death

9.   Why is Vivian reluctant to spend the night with Grant?

   A.   She is not yet divorced and her husband might find out.
   B.   She is afraid of commitment.
   C.   She does not want to get pregnant.
   D.   Neither of them lives alone.

10. Why does Miss Emma hit Jefferson during her visit to his cell?

    A.   He spits on Reverend Ambrose.

    B.   He tells her that he is only a hog being fattened up for the slaughter.

    C.   He throws her food on the ground.

    D.   He insults Vivian.

11. Why does Miss Emma want to meet with Jefferson in the dayroom?

    A.   She thinks the sun will do him good.

    B.   She needs a table on which to serve him food.

    C.   There is no room to sit down in his cell.

    D.   She is afraid to be with him in a confined space.

12. Why didn't Vivian's family like her husband?

    A.   Because he was poor

    B.   Because he was a common laborer

    C.   Because he was dark-skinned

    D.   Because he was prone to drinking

13. What event directly follows the superintendent's visit?

    A.   The arrival of wood for the winter

    B.   The final confirmation of Jefferson's execution date

    C.   The Christmas program

    D.   Grant's mental breakdown

14. How does Grant gather enough money to buy Jefferson a radio?

    A.   He borrows from the Claibornes and several other people at the Rainbow Club.

    B.   He saves for over a month.

    C.   He asks Vivian for it.

    D.   He takes it from Miss Emma's savings.

15. How do Tante Lou and Miss Emma get Grant to visit Jefferson alone?

    A.   By offering to pay him
    B.   By insisting that Miss Emma is ill
    C.   By appealing to Vivian for help
    D.   By talking to the superintendent

16. Sheriff Guidry warns Grant that he will lose his visiting privileges if which of the following happens?

    A.   There is any sign of aggravation in Jefferson
    B.   He doesn't agree to help Guidry control Jefferson
    C.   His wife leaves town
    D.   He continues to disrespect the deputies

17. What do Grant's students send Jefferson?

    A.   A bag of marbles
    B.   A bag of peanuts and pecans
    C.   A small radio
    D.   A birthday card

18. At the Christmas program, Reverend Ambrose makes a subtle reference to which of the following?

    A.   Grant's faithlessness
    B.   Jefferson's false imprisonment
    C.   Miss Emma's illness
    D.   The state of the church

19. Why does Grant get in a fight with two mulatto men in a bar?

    A.   They call Vivian a whore.
    B.   They call him a nigger.
    C.   They gloat over Jefferson's fate.
    D.   They run into him when he is in a foul mood.

20. Jefferson admits to Grant that he would like his last meal to be which of the following?

   A. A gallon of vanilla ice cream
   B. A bucket of his godmother's fried chicken
   C. A giant steak
   D. A glass of water

21. How does Grant get Jefferson's notebook?

   A. He asks the sheriff for it after the execution.
   B. He finds it on the ground outside Jefferson's cell.
   C. Paul delivers it to him.
   D. Tante Lou brings it to his classroom.

22. How does the chair arrive at the courthouse?

   A. On a covered truck
   B. On an old wagon
   C. In the back of a converted hearse
   D. In a huge crate labeled "Produce"

23. What does the sheriff do the morning of Jefferson's execution?

   A. He takes a long bath.
   B. He asks Grant to attend the proceedings.
   C. He eats a big breakfast.
   D. He fires Paul.

24. Who shaves Jefferson before the execution?

   A. Murphy
   B. The executioner
   C. Sheriff Guidry
   D. Grant

25. Who informs Grant that the execution is over?

   A. Paul the deputy
   B. The executioner
   C. Sheriff Guidry
   D. Tante Lou

Suggestions for Further Reading

CARMEAN, KAREN. *Ernest J. Gaines: A Critical Companion.* Westport, Connecticut: Greenwood Press, 1998.

ESTES, DAVID C., ed. *Critical Reflections on the Fiction of Ernest J. Gaines.* Athens: University of Georgia Press, 1994.

GAINES, ERNEST J. *A Gathering of Old Men.* New York: Vintage Press, 1983.

———. *The Autobiography of Miss Jane Pittman.* New York: Dial Press, 1971.

GENOVESE, EUGENE. *Roll, Jordan, Roll: The World the Slaves Made.* New York: Random House, 1993.

PREJEAN, C. S. J. *Dead Man Walking.* New York: Harper and Row, 1991.

ROSENGARTEN, THEODORE. *All God's Dangers: The Life of Nate Shaw.* New York: Broadway Books, 1989.